LINES ON THE UNDERGROUND

*an anthology
for Northern Line travellers*

Compiled by

DOROTHY MEADE & TATIANA WOLFF

*Illustrated by Basil Cottle
and Jonathan Newdick*

CASSELL

To Joe, Dora, Anna and Ben

*

And in memory of
M. M. W.

Cassell Publishers Limited
Wellington House, 125 Strand
London WC2R 0BB

in association with the London Transport Museum

This edition published 1996
The material in this anthology was first published in
Lines on the Underground, 1994

British Library Cataloguing in Publication Data
A catalogue record for this book is available from the British Library

ISBN 0-304-34859-7

Distributed in Australia by
Capricorn Link (Australia) Pty Ltd
2/13 Carrington Road, Castle Hill, NSW 2154

Printed and bound in Great Britain by Hillman Printers Ltd

NORTHERN LINE

Morden

The Morden extension was opened [1926] by Col. J.T. Moore-Brabazon MP, Parliamentary Secretary to the Minister of Transport. He drove the special train from Clapham South to Morden. There was the usual official lunch – held in the car sheds, where the tables were decorated with red and white carnations. . . . To encourage travel on the new line 15,000 free tickets were issued to people living near each station.

DENNIS EDWARDS AND RON PIGRAM, *London's Underground Suburbs*, 1986

South Wimbledon

. . . actually, one bright morning, in full view of the ten-past-ten train from Basingstoke, Monson's flying machine started on its journey.

They saw the carrier running swiftly along its rail, and the white and gold screw spinning in the air. They heard the rapid rumble of wheels, and thud as the carrier reached the buffers at the end of its run. Then a whirr as the Flying-Machine was shot forward into the networks. All that the majority of them had seen and heard before. The thing went with a drooping flight through the framework and rose again, and then every beholder shouted, or screamed, or yelled, or shrieked after his kind. For instead of the customary concussion and stoppage, the Flying-Machine flew out of its five years' cage like a bolt from a crossbow, and drove slantingly upward into the air, curved round a little, so as to cross the line, and soared in the direction of Wimbledon Common. . . .

That was what the people in the train from Basingstoke saw. If you had drawn a line down the middle of that train, from engine to guard's van, you would not have found a living soul on the opposite side to the Flying-Machine. It was a mad rush from window to window as the thing crossed the line. And the engine-driver and stoker never took their eyes off the low hills about Wimbledon, and never noticed that they had run clean through Coombe and Malden and Raynes Park, until, with returning animation, they found themselves pelting, at the most indecent pace, into Wimbledon station.

H.G. WELLS, 'The Argonauts of the Air', *The Plattner Story, and Others*, 1897

Colliers Wood

In 1881 [Willam Morris's] firm moved its works from Queen Square to Merton Abbey [near Colliers Wood]. The works at Merton had originally been a silk-weaving factory, started early in the eighteenth century by Huguenot refugees. . . . At Merton he had the advantage of the river Wandle, a clear and beautiful stream supplying water of the special quality required for madder dyeing. The river-side and the mill-pond were thickly set with willows and large poplars. . . . The whole thing was, in fact, the realization of a Ruskinian dream. . . .

To reach Merton from Hammersmith, Morris had to go by Underground railway to Farringdon Street, cross the City, and then get another train from Ludgate Hill, a journey which took about two hours.

The Letters of William Morris to His Family and Friends
edited by Philip Henderson, 1950

Tooting Broadway

Certainly [Thomas Hardy] advanced socially, elected to both the Savile and the Rabelais Clubs, and meeting such leading figures as Tennyson, Browning, Arnold and Henry James. But he would lie awake in his Upper Tooting house, feeling the 'close proximity to a monster whose body had four million heads and eight million eyes'.

EVELYN L. EVANS, *The Homes of Thomas Hardy*, 1968

Tooting Bec

Lavender Sweep is drowned in Wandsworth,
    Drowned in jessamine up to the neck,
Beetles sway upon bending grass leagues
    Shoulder-level to Tooting Bec.
Rich as Middlesex, rich in signboards,
    Lie the lover-trod lanes between,
Red Man, Green Man, Horse and Waggoner,
    Elms and sycamores round a green.

Burst, good June, with a rush this morning,
Bindweed weave me an emerald rope
Sun, shine bright on the blossoming trellises,
June and lavender, bring me hope.

JOHN BETJEMAN, 'South London Sketch, 1844',
New Bats in Old Belfries, 1945

Balham

Broad-bosomed, bold, becalmed, benign
Lies Bal-ham – four square on the Northern Line.

FRANK MUIR AND DENIS NORDEN 'Balham – Gateway to the South', 1958

In Balham you can buy Greek cheese; yams; Indian mirror cloth; dried fish; black-eyed peas; West African printed cotton sold in 12-yard lengths, sufficient to make a robe; olives in all sizes and colours; every kind of Pakistani sweetmeat; reggae records; hi-life records; canned bamboo shoots; goat; and once I went through the market and did not see a single banana which was neither green nor black. . . .

[My parents] came here in the 1920s because my father worked at nights and tubes run late on the Northern Line. For me, there is a certain inevitability about the place; whenever I've lived in London, it has always been here except for three weeks, once, in Earls Court, when I was running away from home. Nobody runs away from home to Balham because Balham is home.

ANGELA CARTER in *Living in London* edited by Alan Ross, 1974

Clapham South

[Henry] Cavendish, who has been styled 'the Newton of Chemistry', was distinguished as the founder of pneumatic chemistry, and for his successful researches on the composition of water, and his famous experiment, made at Clapham, for the determination of the earth's density. 'The man who weighed the world,' wrote his cousin, the late Duke of Devonshire, in his 'Handbook for Chatsworth', 'buried his science and his wealth in solitude and insignificance at Clapham.'

Almost the whole of his house here was occupied as workshops and laboratory. . . . 'The lawn was invaded by a wooden stage, from which access could be had to a large tree, to the top of which Cavendish, in the course of his astronomical, meteorological, electrical, or other researches, occasionally ascended.'

W. THORNBURY AND E. WALFORD, *Old and New London*, 1873–8

Clapham Common

23 September 1700. I went to visit Mr. Pepys at Clapham, where he has a very noble and wonderfully well-furnish'd house, especially with India and Chinese curiosities. The offices and gardens well accommodated for pleasure and retirement.

26 May 1703. This day died Mr. Sam. Pepys, a very worthy, industrious and curious person, none in England exceeding him in knowledge of the Navy. . . . When K[ing] James II went out of England, he laid down his office and would serve no more, but withdrawing himself from all public affaires, he liv'd at Clapham with his partner Mr. Hewer, formerly his clerk, in a very noble house and sweete place, where he enjoy'd the fruite of his labours in great prosperity. He was universally belov'd, hospitable, generous, learned in many things, skill'd in music, a very greate cherisher of learned men of whom he had the conversation.

JOHN EVELYN, *Diary* quoted in *Memoirs, Illustrative of the Life and Writings of John Evelyn*, 1818

On November 13, 1895 I was brought down here from London. From two o'clock till half-past two on that day I had to stand on the centre platform of Clapham Junction in convict dress and handcuffed, for the world to look at. I had been taken out of the Hospital Ward without a moment's notice being given to me. Of all possible objects I was the most grotesque. When people saw me they laughed. Each train as it came up swelled the audience. Nothing could exceed their amusement. That was, of course, before they knew who I was. As soon as they had been informed, they laughed still more. For half an hour I stood there in the grey November rain surrounded by a jeering mob.

OSCAR WILDE, *De Profundis*, 1905

Clapham North

[Mrs Newcome's] mansion at Clapham was long the resort of the most favoured amongst the religious world. The most eloquent expounders, the most gifted missionaries, the most interesting converts from foreign islands, were to be found at her sumptuous table, spread with the produce of her magnificent gardens. Heaven indeed blessed those gardens with plenty, as many reverend gentlemen remarked; there were no finer grapes, peaches, or pineapples in all England.

WILLIAM MAKEPEACE THACKERAY, *The Newcomes*, 1853–5

By the zeal, the munificence, the laborious activity, with which [the Clapham Sect] pursued their religious and semi-religious enterprises, they did more to teach the world how to get rid of existing institutions than by their votes and speeches at Westminster they contributed to preserve them. With their May meetings, and African Institutions, and Anti-Slavery Reporters, and their subscriptions of tens of thousands of pounds, and their petitions bristling with hundreds of thousands of signatures, and all the machinery for informing opinion and bringing it to bear on ministers and legislators which they did so much to perfect and even to invent, they can be regarded as nothing short of pioneers and fuglemen of that system of popular agitation which forms a leading feature in our internal history during the past half-century.

G.O. TREVELYAN, *The Life and Letters of Lord Macaulay*, 1876

Stockwell
Change for Victoria line

In 1778 [Stockwell] was alarmed by an apparition, known to this day as 'the Stockwell Ghost', which spread such terror through the then retired village and neighbourhood. . . . This story is thus told by Charles Mackay in his *Extraordinary Popular Delusions* – 'Mrs Golding, an elderly lady, who resides alone with her servant, Anne Robinson, was sorely surprised, on the evening of the Twelfth Day, 1772, to observe an extraordinary commotion among the crockery. Cups and saucers rattled down the chimney, pots and pans were whirled downwards or through the windows; and hams, cheeses, and loaves of bread disported themselves upon the floor just as if the devil were in them. . . .

'It appears that Anne was anxious to have a clear house to carry on an intrigue with her lover, and she resorted to this trick in order to effect her purpose. She placed the china on the shelves in such a manner that it fell on the slightest motion; and she attached horse-hair to other articles, so that she could jerk them down from the adjoining room without being perceived by anyone.'

W. THORNBURY AND E. WALFORD, *Old and New London*, 1873–8

Oval

The Oval is green,
Flats, gnats,
And white-clothed figures move with grace,
The bat and ball!
These above all,
And the thrill, and the air of this place!

The sound of applause,
Lunch, crunch,
And the sudden dejected roar,
The light and the sight
Of Learie's old might,
The Pavilion's clamour for more!

More of this man!
Run! Run!
O run, Learie! run while you may!
A fight is in sight
And the play has a bite
It's a *wonderful* Oval day!

LESLIE FREWIN, 'On Seeing Sir Learie Constantine return (temporarily) from Diplomacy to Cricket, September 1963', *The Poetry of Cricket* edited by Leslie Frewin

At the Oval, men seem to have rushed away with some zest from their City offices. At Lord's, there is a *dilettante* look, as of men whose work, if ever, has yet to come.

JAMES PYCROFT, *Oxford Memories*, 1886

Kennington
Change for Bank branch
Turn to page 14 for Elephant and Castle

Mother, Sydney and I looked a crumpled sight as we ambled out through the workhouse gates. It was early morning and we had nowhere to go, so we walked to Kennington Park, which was about a mile away. Sydney had ninepence tied up in a handkerchief, so we bought half a pound of black cherries and spent the morning in Kennington Park, sitting on a bench eating them. Sydney crumpled a sheet of newspaper and wrapped some string around it and for a while the three of us played catch-ball. At noon we went to a coffee-shop and spent the rest of our money on a twopenny tea-cake, a penny bloater and two halfpenny cups of tea, which we shared between us. Afterwards we returned to the park where Sydney and I played again while Mother sat crocheting.

In the afternoon we made our way back to the workhouse.

CHARLIE CHAPLIN, *My Autobiography*, 1964

CHARING CROSS BRANCH
Waterloo
Change for Bakerloo line

. . . on Waterloo Bridge. . . . The wind has blown up the waves. The river races beneath us, and the men standing on the barges have to lean all their weight on the tiller. A black tarpaulin is tied down over a swelling load of gold. Avalanches of coal glitter blackly. As usual, painters are slung on planks across the great riverside hotels, and the hotel windows have already points of light in them. On the other side the city is white as if with age; St. Paul's swells white above the fretted, pointed, or oblong buildings beside it. The cross alone shines rosy-gilt.

VIRGINIA WOOLF, *Jacob's Room*, 1922

. . . exclaimed Sam [Weller] '. . . I had unfurnished lodgin's for a fort-night . . . the dry arches of Waterloo Bridge. Fine sleeping place – within ten minutes' walk of all the public offices – only if there is any objection to it, it is that the sitivation's *rayther* too airy. I see some queer sights there.'

CHARLES DICKENS, *The Pickwick Papers*, 1836–7

Embankment

Change for Bakerloo, Circle and District lines

If you can put up with the thunderous noise of the trains close to your backside, the sight of the Thames from the gangway across Hungerford Bridge is one of the finest in London, especially when the wind lifts the water into wavelets. It is Canaletto come alive.

JOHN HILLABY, *John Hillaby's London*, 1987

Charing Cross

Change for Bakerloo and Jubilee lines

1775. I talked of the cheerfulness of Fleet Street, owing to the constant quick succession of people which we perceive passing through it. JOHNSON. 'Why, Sir, Fleet Street has a very animated appearance; but I think the full tide of human existence is at Charing Cross.'

1777. I had long complained to him that I felt myself discontented in Scotland, as too narrow a sphere, and that I wished to make my chief residence in London, the great scene of ambition, instruction, and amusement; a scene which was to me, comparatively speaking, a heaven upon earth. JOHNSON. 'Why, Sir, I never knew anyone who had such a *gust* for London as you have; and I cannot blame you for your wish to live there.'

I suggested a doubt, that if I were to reside in London, the exquisite zest with which I relished it in occasional visits might go off, and I might grow tired of it. JOHNSON. 'Why, Sir, you find no man, at all intellectual, who is willing to leave London. No, Sir, when a man is tired of London, he is tired of life; for there is in London all that life can afford.'

JAMES BOSWELL, *The Life of Samuel Johnson*, 1791

The Charing Cross trains rumbled through my dreams on one side, the boom of the Strand on the other, while before my windows, Father Thames under the Shot Tower walked up and down with his traffic.*

*Kipling was in lodgings in Villiers Street, off the Strand.

RUDYARD KIPLING, *Something of Myself*, 1889

Leicester Square
Change for Piccadilly line

Sir Joshua Reynolds 'At Home' at Leicester Square: It was no prim, fine table he set them down to. There was little order or arrangement; there was more abundance than elegance; and a happy freedom thrust conventionalism aside. Often was the dinner-board, prepared for seven or eight, required to accommodate itself to fifteen or sixteen; for often on the very eve of dinner, would Sir Joshua tempt afternoon visitors with intimation that Johnson, or Garrick, or Goldsmith was to dine there. Nor was the want of seats the only difficulty. A want of knives and forks, of plates and glasses, as often succeeded . . . it was easy to know the guests well acquainted with the house by their never failing to call instantly for beer, bread, or wine, that they might get them before the first course was over, and the worst confusion began.

JOHN FORSTER, *The Life and Adventures of Oliver Goldsmith*, 1848

His [Sir Joshua Reynolds's] study was octagonal. . . . His sitter's chair moved on castors, and stood above the floor a foot and a half. He held his palettes by a handle, and the sticks of his brushes were eighteen inches long. He wrought standing, and with great celerity. He rose early, breakfasted at nine, entered his study at ten, examined designs or touched unfinished portraits till eleven brought a sitter; painted till four; then dressed, and gave the evening to company.

ALLAN CUNNINGHAM, *The Lives of the Most Eminent British Painters, Sculptors and Architects*, 1829–33

. . . that curious region lying about the Haymarket and Leicester Square, which is a centre of attraction to indifferent foreign hotels and indifferent foreigners, racket-courts, fighting-men, swordsmen, foot-guards, old china, gaming houses, exhibitions, and a large medley of shabbiness and shrinking out of sight.

CHARLES DICKENS, *Bleak House*, 1852–3

We four kings of Leicester Square
Selling ladies' underwear:
　How fantastic!
　No elastic!
Only 15p per pair.

'Children's Rhymes' quoted in *London in Verse* edited by
Christopher Logue, 1982

Tottenham Court Road
Change for Central line

John Forster quotes this comment by Charles Dickens on his boyhood experiences on the way to work from his home in Gower Street to the blacking factory at Hungerford-stairs: 'I could not resist the stale pastry put out at half-price on trays at the confectioners' doors in Tottenham-court-road, and I often spent in that the money I should have kept for my dinner.'

JOHN FORSTER, *The Life of Charles Dickens*, 1872–4

Some, by the banks of *Thame* their pleasure taking;
Some, Sulli-bibs among the Milk-maids, making;
With musique, some upon the waters, rowing;
Some, to the next adjoyning Hamlets going;
And *Hogsdone, Islington,* and *Tothnam-Court,*
For Cakes and Creame, had then no small resort.

GEORGE WITHER, *Britain's Remembrancer,* 1628

Goodge Street

It appears . . . that the members of the [London Explorers'] Club take coach trips all round London and are enthusiastic about everything they see. . . . How much livelier a city London would be if charabanc-loads of its citizens were constantly passing through its streets and if, when they came, say, to Goodge Street, and somebody called out: 'Three cheers for Goodge Street!' and the company responded with a shout! I doubt whether Goodge Street has ever been cheered in the course of its history.

ROBERT LYND, *Searchlights and Nightingales,* 1939

It seemed a perpetual adventure to buy second-hand books in the Charing Cross Road, or drink in the Swiss Pub or the York Minster or stand outside Goodge Street Underground Station in that long silence, filled with infinite possibilities, between the moment when the buzz-bombs cut off and the thud as they fell somewhere else.

JOHN MORTIMER, *Clinging to the Wreckage,* 1982

Warren Street

Change for Victoria line
Turn to page 17 for Euston

Sunday, 20 October 1940. The most – what? – impressive, no, that's not it – sight in London on Friday was the queue, mostly children with suitcases, outside Warren St tube. This was about 11.30. We thought they were evacuees, waiting for a bus. But there they were, in a much longer line, with women, men, more bags & blankets, sitting still at 3. Lining up for the shelter in the night's raid – which came of course.

VIRGINIA WOOLF, *Diary,* Vol. V, 1936–41

CITY BRANCH

Elephant & Castle
Change for Bakerloo line

By the cloisterly Temple, and by Whitefriars . . . and by Blackfriars-bridge, and Blackfriars-road, Mr. George sedately marches to a street of little shops lying somewhere in that ganglion of roads from Kent and Surrey, and of streets from the bridges of London, centring in the far-famed Elephant who has lost his Castle formed of a thousand four-horse coaches, to a stronger iron monster than he, ready to chop him into mince-meat any day he dares. To one of the little shops in this street, which is a musician's shop, having a few fiddles in the window, and some Pan's pipes and a tambourine, and a triangle, and certain elongated scraps of music, Mr. George directs his massive tread. And halting at a few paces from it, as he sees a soldierly looking woman, with her outer skirts tucked up, come forth with a small wooden tub, and in that tub commence a whisking and a splashing on the margin of the pavement, Mr. George says to himself, 'She's as usual, washing greens. I never saw her, except upon a baggage-wagon, when she wasn't washing greens!'

CHARLES DICKENS, *Bleak House*, 1852–3

Borough

Once the main road to the south and the terminus for coaches when London Bridge was too narrow to carry them into the city. In the 17th century, according to Thomas Dekker, it was full of inns, 'a continued ale house with not a shop to be seen between'.

The London Encyclopaedia edited by Ben Weinreb and Christopher Hibbert, 1983

Went to the Borough yesterday morning before going to Gadshill, to see if I could find any ruins of the Marshalsea. Found a great part of the original building – now 'Marshalsea Place'. Found the rooms that have been in my mind's eye in the story. Found, nursing a very big boy, a very small boy*, who, seeing me standing on the Marshalsea pavement, looking about, told me how it all used to be. God knows how he learned it (for he was a world too young to know anything about it), but he was right enough.

* In his Preface to the first edition of *Little Dorrit* in 1857, Dickens describes this same inci-

dent and says of this boy: 'the smallest boy I ever conversed with, carrying the largest baby I ever saw, offered a supernaturally intelligent explanation of the locality in its old uses, and was very nearly correct.'

CHARLES DICKENS, 1856, quoted in *The Life of Charles Dickens*
by John Forster, 1872–4

London Bridge

London Bridge is broken down,
Broken down, broken down,
London Bridge is broken down,
My fair lady.

Nursery Rhyme, *c.*1726

[William] Hogarth's studio [on London Bridge] resembled one of the alchemist's laboratories from the pencil of the elder Teniers. It was a complete, smoke-stained confusionary, with a German stove, crucibles, pipkins, and nests of drawers with rings of twine to pull them out; here a box of asphaltum, there glass-stoppered bottles, varnishes, dabbers, gravers, etching tools, walls of wax, obsolete copper-plates, many engraved on both sides, and poetry scribbled over the walls; a pallet hung up as an heir-loom, the colours dry upon it, hard as stone; all the multifarious *arcanalia* of engraving, and lastly, a Printing Press!

JOHN TIMBS, *Romance of London*, 1865

Bank
Change for Central line and for escalator to Monument station
for Circle and District lines

During the formidable riots of 1780 the Bank was in considerable danger. In one night there rose the flames of six-and-twenty fires. Newgate was sacked and burned. The mob, half thieves, at last decided to march upon the Bank, but precautions had been taken there. The courts and roof of the building were defended by armed clerks and volunteers, and there were soldiers ready outside. The old pewter inkstands had been melted into bullets. The rioters made two rushes; the first was checked by a volley from the soldiers; at the second, which was less violent, Wilkes rushed out, and with his own hand dragged in some of the ringleaders. Leaving several killed and many wounded, the discomfited mob at last retired.

W. THORNBURY AND E. WALFORD, *Old and New London*, 1873–8

Moorgate
Change for Circle, Hammersmith & City and Metropolitan lines

A plaque at No. 85 Moorgate near its junction with London Wall in the City marks the site of [John Keats'] birthplace, a livery stable run by his father.

IAN OUSBY, *Literary Britain and Ireland*, 1990

Old Street

'The choicest fruits of the kingdom were reared in King James I's time by John Milton, in his Nursery in Old Street.'

Oldys on Trees [MS] quoted by H.B. Wheatley
in *London Past and Present*, 1891

Angel

[In the eighteenth century] a bell was rung periodically at the Angel, Islington, to announce the departure of a convoy of foot passengers across the fields to the City. They gathered at the end of St John Street and were escorted into the precincts of the City by an armed patrol.

CHRISTOPHER TRENT, *Greater London*, 1965

The City and South London was the first real 'tube' electric railway, and it still had, when I first knew it, the atmosphere of 1890, the year of its opening. Little orange engines carried rolling stock, with basket seats and cut glass electric lights. Many of the platforms, still to be seen at Angel, Kings Cross and south of the river, were central and narrow, with trains running either side of them. . . . The whole railway had a strong smell of wet feet or a changing room after games and the line was delightfully uneven, so that one could look down the length of the carriages and see them switchbacking up and down, behind or before one.

JOHN BETJEMAN, 'Coffee, Port and Cigars on the Inner Circle', *The Times*, 24 May 1963

King's Cross St. Pancras
Change for Circle, Hammersmith & City, Metropolitan, Piccadilly
and Victoria lines

[The Midland Railway] tunnelled one line down to join the Metropolitan (steam) Underground Railway, which is now part of the Inner Circle. . . . Much of the trade of the line was beer from Burton-on-Trent, and the distance between the columns was measured by the length of beer barrels, which were carried down here from the station above by hydraulic lifts, and taken by drays out into London. . . . The hotel . . . was opened to the public in 1873. At the time it was easily the most magnificent of all London hotels. It was one of the first to have lifts, called 'ascending rooms' and worked by hydraulic power. It was also one of the first to have electric bells.

JOHN BETJEMAN, *London's Historic Railway Stations*, 1972

Euston
Change for Victoria line

How long ago Hector took off his plume,
Not wanting that his little son should cry,
Then kissed his sad Andromache goodbye –
And now we three in Euston waiting-room.

FRANCES CORNFORD, 'Parting in Wartime',
Travelling Home, 1948

Mornington Crescent
Temporarily closed

There was a few years ago a month of June which [Spencer Frederick] Gore verily seems to have used as if he had known that it was to be for him the last of its particularly fresh and sumptuous kind. He used to look down on the garden of Mornington Crescent. The trained trees rise and droop in fringes, like fountains, over the little well of greenness and shade where parties of young people are playing at tennis. The backcloth is formed by the tops of the brown houses in the Hampstead Road, and the liver-coloured tiles of the Tube station.

WALTER SICKERT, 'A Perfect Modern', *New Age*, 9 April 1914,
after Gore's death

Camden Town

Change for Mill Hill & Barnet branch of Northern line
Turn to page 25 for Kentish Town

From the geyser ventilators
  Autumn winds are blowing down
On a thousand business women
  Having baths in Camden Town.

Waste pipes chuckle into runnels,
  Steam's escaping here and there,
Morning trains through Camden cutting
  Shake the Crescent and the Square.
Early nip of changeful autumn,
  Dahlias glimpsed through garden doors,
At the back precarious bathrooms
  Jutting out from upper floors;

And behind their frail partitions
  Business women lie and soak,
Seeing through the draughty skylight
  Flying clouds and railway smoke.

Rest you there, poor unbelov'd ones,
  Lap your loneliness in heat.
All too soon the tiny breakfast,
  Trolley-bus and windy street!

JOHN BETJEMAN, 'Business Girls',
A Few Late Chrysanthemums, 1954

The first shock of a great earthquake had, just at that period, rent the whole neighbourhood. Houses were knocked down; streets broken through and stopped; deep pits and trenches dug in the ground; enormous heaps of earth and clay thrown up; buildings that were undermined and shaking, propped by great beams of wood. Here, a chaos of carts, overthrown and jumbled together, lay topsy-turvy at the bottom of a steep, unnatural hill; there, confused treasures of iron soaked and rusted in something that had accidentally become a pond.

Everywhere were bridges that led nowhere; thoroughfares that were wholly impassable; Babel towers of chimneys, wanting half their height; temporary wooden houses and enclosures, in the most unlikely situations; carcases of ragged tenements, and fragments of unfinished walls and arches, and piles of scaffolding, and wildernesses of bricks, and giant forms of cranes, and tripods straddling above nothing. . . . In short, the yet unfinished and unopened Railroad was in progress.

CHARLES DICKENS, *Dombey and Son*, 1847–8

EDGWARE BRANCH

Chalk Farm

Some farmers farm in fruit, some farm in grain,
　　Others farm in dairy-stuff, and many farm in vain,
But I know a place for a Sunday morning's walk
Where the Farmer and his Family only farm in chalk.
The Farmer and his Family before you walk back
Will bid you in to sit awhile and share their mid-day snack –
O they that live in Chalk Farm they live at their ease,
For the Farmer and his Family can't tell chalk from cheese.

ELEANOR FARJEON, *Nursery Rhymes of London Town*, 1916

Belsize Park

BELLSIZE HOUSE

There is now the best Diversion in the Park that hath been yet; for the Proprietor hath actually got a great many Wild Deer, and will hunt one down every Thursday and Saturday, and kill it fairly before the Company. For that purpose he hath enlarged his Pack of Hounds, which will shew good Diversion for Two or Three Hours. The Hunting will begin exactly at Four of the Clock. And for the Conveniency of single Gentlemen, there will be a very good Ordinary, exactly at Two a Clock, and one of the Dishes will always be a Venison Pasty. And on the By-Days, every Eve'ning, there will be good Sport shew'd in the Canals. And there will be a Scaffold erected there for the Musick to play, whilst the Gentlemen and Ladies are Walking there. The Walks round are made very commodious. And for the Safety of the Company, the Proprietor hath hired Twenty stout labouring Men, well known about Hampstead, to line the road betwixt Bellsize and London; so that they will be safe to pass as well by Night as Day.

Daily Post, 5 June 1722

One evening after dinner in a restaurant with some friends we returned home by Underground taking the Northern Line to Belsize Park. As a rule I went into town by car and I hadn't been by Tube for ages. For the first time that evening I saw people lying on the platforms at all the stations we stopped at. . . . I had never seen so many reclining figures and even the train tunnels seemed to be like the holes in my sculpture. And amid the grim tension, I noticed groups of strangers formed together in intimate groups and children asleep within feet of the passing trains. After this evening I travelled all over London by Underground. . . . I never made sketches in the Underground. It would have been like drawing in the hold of a slave ship. I would wander about sometimes passing a particular group that interested me half a dozen times. Sometimes, in a corner where I could not be seen, I would make notes on the back of an envelope so that I would be reminded when I sketched next day.

HENRY MOORE, *Shelter Sketchbook*, 1940, quoted in *London Under London* by Richard Trench and Ellis Hillman, 1984, revised 1993

Hampstead

'Tis so near heaven, that I dare not say it can be a proper situation, for any but a race of mountaineers.

DANIEL DEFOE, *A Tour thro' the Whole Island of Great Britain*, 1928 edition

'You don't feel disposed, do you, to muffle yourself up, and start off with me for a good brisk walk over Hampstead-heath? I knows a good 'ous there where we can have a red hot chop for dinner and a glass of good wine': which led to our first experience of Jack Straw's-castle, memorable for many happy meetings in coming years.

CHARLES DICKENS, letter, 1837, in *The Life of Charles Dickens* by John Forster, 1872–4

Hampstead . . . offers the perfect fusion of urban bustle and rural privacy, as if all the elements of English townscape had been tossed in the air and fallen on this hillside with hardly a piece out of place. The people of Hampstead – pump-room rowdies, 'Bohemian' commuters, left-wing intellectuals – are merely its passing phantoms. The lasting Hampstead is a maze of steps, alleyways, turnings and sudden views. It is sprays of clematis, wisteria, ivy and holly scattering sunlight on to red brick and white stucco. It is grand mansions, terraced cottages, Victorian extravagance and workhouse simplicity contained within a surprisingly intact eighteenth- and nineteenth-century hill town, defended on three sides by a rambling heath and on the fourth by the stern ramparts of Italianate Belsize Park. The twentieth century has lobbed an occasional grenade over these ramparts. But Hampstead's defenders have become increasingly adept at lobbing them back. For once, it is probable that the town we see today is the town we shall bequeath to our descendants.

SIMON JENKINS, *The Companion Guide to Outer London*, 1981

The station platforms at Hampstead [the deepest in London] are 192 feet under the surface – as far below ground as Nelson is above it in Trafalgar Square.

HUGH DOUGLAS, *The Underground Story*, 1963

It was something of an adventure for Lady Slane to go alone to Hampstead, and she felt happier after safely changing trains at Charing Cross. . . . Yet, going up to Hampstead alone, she did not feel old; she felt younger than she had felt for years, and the proof of it was that she accepted eagerly this start of a new lap in life, even though it be the last. Nor did she look her age, as she sat, swaying slightly with the rocking of the Underground train, very upright, clasping her umbrella and her bag, her ticket carefully pushed into the opening of her glove. . . .

The train itself came to her assistance, for, after jerking over points, it ran into yet another white-tiled station, where a line of red tiles framed the name: Hampstead. Lady Slane rose unsteadily to her feet, reaching out her hand for a helpful bar; it was on these occasions and these alone, when she must compete with the rush of mechanical life, that she betrayed herself for an old lady. . . .

It was a wonder, arrived at Hampstead, that Lady Slane descended from the train in time, successfully clasping her umbrella, her bag, and her ticket inside her glove, but descend she did, and found herself standing in the warm summer air with the roofs of London beneath her. The passers-by ignored her, standing there, so well accustomed were they to the sight of old ladies in Hampstead. Setting out to walk, she wondered if she remembered the way; but Hampstead seemed scarcely a part of London, so sleepy and village-like, with its warm red-brick houses and vistas of trees and distance that reminded her pleasantly of Constable's paintings.

V. SACKVILLE-WEST, *All Passion Spent*, 1931

Golders Green

I was four years old when my father built his house in what was then the village of North End, Hampstead. He was, in fact, the first of its spoliators. When we settled there the tube reached no further than Hampstead. Golders Green was a grassy cross-road with a sign pointing to London, Finchley and Hendon; such a place as where 'the Woman in White' was encountered. All round us lay dairy farms, market gardens and a few handsome old houses in brick or stucco standing in twenty acres or more; not far off there survived woods where we picked bluebells, and streams beside which we opened our picnic baskets. North End Road was a steep, dusty lane with white posts and rails bordering its footways. North End, the reader may remember, was the place where Bill Sikes spent the first night of his flight after the murder of Nancy. . . .

. . . Eventually (I think soon after the first war) our postal address was altered from Hampstead to Golders Green. My father deplored the change, because Hampstead had historic associations, with Keats and Blake and Constable, while Golders Green meant, to him, merely a tube station.

EVELYN WAUGH, *A Little Learning*, 1964

Brent Cross

Brent Cross – a name which has come to symbolise the consumer society in car-owning, TV-watching, wine-drinking, mortgage-paying, credit card postwar Britain – is 10 years old tomorrow. Morris dancers, 'ethnic dancers', Tottenham Hotspurs, hot air balloons and a competition for the capital's worst-dressed man will celebrate its birthday in what foreigners will regard as inimitably Anglo-Saxon style.

The Times, third leader, 12 July 1986

Hendon Central

In the fourteenth century the manor of Hendon was in the gift of Westminster Abbey. During the Black Death the area became a haven. Cattle from other places were transported on the hoof, accompanied by one or two grangers, and were retained here till the worst of the plague was over.

The London Encyclopaedia edited by Ben Weinreb
and Christopher Hibbert, 1983

So obese is my cousin from Hendon,
She looks elephantine, seen end on;
What preys most on her mind
Is her efforts to find
A good deck-chair that she can depend on.

A.H. BAYNES, *Penguin Book of Limericks* edited by E.O. Parrott, 1983

Our Farnham which art in Hendon
Holloway Turnpike Lane
Thy Kingston come
Thy Wimbledon
In Erith as it is in Hendon.
Give us this day our Maidenhead . . .
And lead us not into Penge station
But deliver us from Esher
For thine is the Kingston
The Tower and the Horley
For Iver and Iver
Crouch End.

Schoolboy apocryphal

Colindale

Near Colindale Station . . . is the British Museum newspaper repository. Within, the atmosphere is one of calm: one can obtain a temporary ticket for a day's research, with access to vast stocks of newspapers, extensive catalogues and elaborate indexes. In its reading rooms there is little sound save for the turning of yellowed leaves, and the occasional rumble of a trolley as the attendant delivers two or three elephant folios of newspapers, which are propped up on great reading stands.

BRUCE STEVENSON, *Middlesex,* 1972

Burnt Oak

Burnt Oak, Theydon Bois and Headstone Lane have names that whisper promises of wide open spaces and smiling, unsullied countryside. They are all stations on the London Underground system.

PHILIP HOWARD, *The Times*

The name probably derives from the Roman custom of burning a tree to mark a boundary. Until 1920 the area was mainly farmland, well-wooded and with the Silk Stream running through to Brent. . . . One of the area's principal public houses, the Bald Faced Stag, was a famous coaching inn patronised by generations of travellers from the north.

The London Encyclopaedia edited by Ben Weinreb
and Christopher Hibbert, 1983

Edgware

In this Road [Edgworth Road] lyes the Town of Edgworth, some will have it that it was built by King Edgar the Saxon Monarch, and called by his name, and so will have the town called Edgar, and that it was built as a garrison on the said Watling-Street, to preserve the high-way from thieves: But all this I take to be fabulous, and without authority.

DANIEL DEFOE, *A Tour thro' the Whole Island of Great Britain,* 1928 edition

Edgware. . . . The blacksmith's shop is that in which, according to tradition, worked the musical blacksmith, whose performance on the anvil whilst Handel took shelter from a shower, suggested to the great musician the well-known melody named after him.

JAMES THORNE, *Handbook to the Environs of London*, 1876

BARNET AND MILL HILL EAST BRANCHES

Kentish Town

There will soon be one street from London to Brentford; ay, and from London to every village ten miles round! Lord Camden has just let ground at Kentish Town for building fourteen hundred houses – nor do I wonder; London is, I am certain, much fuller than ever I saw it. I have twice this spring been going to stop my coach in Piccadilly, to inquire what was the matter, thinking there was a mob – not at all; it was only passengers.

HORACE WALPOLE, letter to the Miss Berrys, 8 June 1791

One day in the early 1970s I was roaming through a particularly disjointed and run-down area of Kentish Town, London NW5, and passed a row of houses which were then occupied by squatters engaged in a cold war with Camden Council. They were – and are – unremarkable houses; a mid-Victorian terrace of the type that has been demolished all over London in the past two decades, with none of the Georgian cottage appeal that might commend them to preservationist forces. In stock brick, three storeys, with a dank basement area below and a parapet wall on top, they faced a busy road; the most quintessentially ordinary houses, you would say, though of a uniquely English kind, built by speculative builders for Philistines, unloved now for decades, doomed soon, perhaps, to extinction.

Then I saw that over the lintel of one of them someone had carefully carved an inscription: the letters, cut through the sooty surface into the fresh yellow brick below, stood out clearly –
        'The Fields Lie Sleeping Underneath.'
It is deeply satisfying to come unexpectedly face to face with your own private vision in this way. For years, walking round London, I had been aware of the actual land, lying concealed but not entirely changed or destroyed, beneath the surface of the nineteenth- and twentieth-century city.

GILLIAN TINDALL, *The Fields Beneath*, 1977

Rumbling under blackened girders, Midland, bound for Cricklewood,
Puffed its sulphur to the sunset where that Land of Laundries stood.
Rumble under, thunder over, train and tram alternate go,
Shake the floor and smudge the ledger, Charrington, Sells, Dale & Co.,
Nuts and nuggets in the window, trucks along the lines below.
. . .
Oh the after-tram-ride quiet, when we heard a mile beyond,
Silver music from the bandstand, barking dogs by Highgate Pond;
Up the hill where stucco houses in Virginia creeper drown –
And my childish wave of pity, seeing children carrying down
Sheaves of drooping dandelions to the courts of Kentish Town.

JOHN BETJEMAN, 'Parliament Hill Fields',
New Bats in Old Belfries, 1945

Jenny Marx, wife of Karl, wrote of their move from Dean Street to Grafton Terrace, Kentish Town, in 1856: '. . . a small house at the foot of romantic Hampstead Heath, not far from lovely Primrose Hill. When we slept in our own beds for the first time, sat on our own chairs and even had a parlour with second-hand furniture, then we really thought we were living in a magic castle.'

ASA BRIGGS, *Marx in London*, 1982

Tufnell Park

According to tradition, Tufnell Park Road is an old Roman road: its straightness makes the story likely. The country atmosphere of the area remained undisturbed for many centuries and, as London extended, this northern part of Islington provided its share of the 'very extensive dairies for supplying the inhabitants of the metropolis with milk' . . . in the early 19th century, the painter J.M.W. Turner was still able to enjoy sketching a group of elms on the Old Roman Road.

The London Encyclopaedia edited by Ben Weinreb
and Christopher Hibbert, 1983

Archway

Work began on the [Archway] tunnel, however, and about 130 yards were completed. In the early hours of 13 April 1812 the tunnel collapsed. The *Sun* newspaper reported it thus: 'Between four and five o'clock yesterday morning, the Highgate tunnel fell in with a tremendous crash, and the labour of several months was, in a few moments, converted into a heap of ruins . . .'

. . . The collapse of the tunnel was a source of satisfaction to the residents of Highgate. Lloyd reprints a splendid travesty of a prospectus for rescuing the project. It is headed 'Proposals for removing Highgate Hill entirely, with the houses thereon'. It goes on to describe how the promoters planned to remove the whole village, chapel and all, and to form a salt-water lake where Highgate once stood from Kentish Town to Finchley.

JOHN RICHARDSON, *Highgate: Its History since the Fifteenth Century*, 1983

This was the old Hampstead and Highgate line (now at the heart of the Northern system) with carriages opening at the ends to swing gates and gatemen shouting the stations. What a clatter and what roaring gales through the tunnels! What strange smells from the dim red-and-white tiled platforms! How uncomfortable the shiny straw seats! My joy was to sit at the very back of the train and watch the bright circle of the station dwindle like a camera-lens stopped down.

G.W. STONIER, *Pictures on the Pavement*, 1955

Highgate

When we came upon Highgate hill and had a view of London, I was all life and joy.

JAMES BOSWELL, *The London Journal*, 19 November 1762

The spot at Highgate Hill, whereon the legend states Whittington stopped when he heard the sound of Bow bells, which he imagined prophesied his becoming Lord Mayor, is believed to have been originally the site of a wayside cross, belonging to the formerly adjacent lazar-house, or hospital, and Chapel of St. Anthony; this memorial was removed, and Whittington is stated to have placed there an obelisk, surmounted by a cross, which remained till 1795, when was erected another stone, which has since been twice renewed.

JOHN TIMBS, *Romance of London*, 1865

Safe, in a world of trains and buttered toast
Where things inanimate could feel and think,
Deeply I loved thee, 31 West Hill!
At that hill's foot did London then begin,
With yellow horse-trams clopping past the planes
To grey-brick nonconformist Chetwynd Road
And on to Kentish Town and barking dogs
And costers' carts and crowded grocers' shops
And Daniels' store, the local Selfridge's,
The Bon Marché, the Electric Palace, slums
That thrilled me with their smells of poverty -
And buttered toast and 31 West Hill.
Here from my eyrie, as the sun went down,
I heard the old North London puff and shunt,
Glad that I did not live in Gospel Oak.

JOHN BETJEMAN, *Summoned by Bells*, 1960

East Finchley

Once a tongue of ice came as far as Finchley, bringing with it boulders of rock from far to the north, as well as clay and finely crushed rock from the lands over which it had travelled. When the ice melted the boulders embedded in clay were left behind in the deposit we know as boulder clay. So it is that we find large lumps of chalk from Lincolnshire in the tongue of boulder clay that today stretches from Whetstone to East Finchley Station.

R.S. FITTER, *London's Natural History*, 1945

Eric Aumonier, who had provided a sculpture for 55 Broadway some ten years earlier, was commissioned to design another. . . . The powerful figure of the 'Archer' aiming in the direction of London symbolizes the rapid transit of modern electric trains and is the most distinctive feature of the station.

LAURENCE MENEAR, *London's Underground Stations*, 1983

Finchley Central

As late as 1790 Finchley Common was dangerous to traverse at night. In that year Sir Gilbert Elliot (by no means a timid man), writes to his wife [in *Life and Letters of Sir Gilbert Elliot*] when within a few stages of London, that instead of pushing on that night, as he easily could, he shall defer his arrival till the morning, for 'I shall not trust my throat on Finchley Common in the dark'.

JAMES THORNE, *Handbook to the Environs of London*, 1876

Finchley Central is two and sixpence
    From Golders Green on the Northern line,
And on the platform, by the kiosk,
    That's where you said you'd be mine.
There we made a date,
    For hours I waited,
    But I'm blowed,
    You never showed;
And Finchley Central ten long stations
    From Golders Green change at Camden Town,
I thought I'd made you, but I'm afraid you
    Only let me down.

GEOFF STEPHENS AND A. KLEIN (of the New Vaudeville Band), 1967

Mill Hill East

In the grounds [of Mill Hill school] . . . is a building known as the 'scriptorium' where James Augustus Henry Murray, a master there from 1870 to 1885, deposited three tons of paper slips, used in the preparation of the *Oxford English Dictionary*. That the 'greatest lexicographical project of the age' was prepared in this village is an inspiring thought.

BRUCE STEVENSON, *Middlesex*, 1972

West Finchley

Lord Finchley tried to mend the Electric Light
Himself. It struck him dead: And serve him right!
It is the business of the wealthy man
To give employment to the artisan.

HILAIRE BELLOC, *More Peers*, 1911

Woodside Park

Woodside Park was recorded as Fyncheley Wode in 1468 and was part of the great Middlesex woodland area, and named Woodside in 1686.

CYRIL M. HARRIS, *What's in a Name?*, 1977

Totteridge & Whetstone

Dick Turpin positively loved this highway and its associations, and his 'Knights of the Road' followed his taste. So great was the terror which they inspired among the wealthier classes, that many Scotch lords and squires preferred to make the journey from their native hills to the Parliament at Westminster by sea, rather than encounter the terrors of the Great North road within ten or twelve miles of London.

E. WALFORD, *Greater London*, 1882–4

High Barnet

April 14, 1471. The battle of Barnet was fought in the wars between the houses of York and Lancaster, and the Earl of Warwick, called 'the king-maker', was slain on the field.

WILLIAM HONE, *The Everyday Book*, 1830

The battlefield [of Barnet] lies direct north of the town. . . . Red Rose met White Rose, and a sorry chapter of our story closed that April morning of 1471, while still the sun was climbing high. . . . An obelisk, erected in 1740, marks the traditional spot where Warwick the King-maker fell.

W.G. BELL, *Where London Sleeps*, 1926

Early on the seventh morning after he had left his native place, Oliver limped slowly into the little town of Barnet. The window-shutters were closed; the street was empty; not a soul had awakened to the business of the day. The sun was rising in all its splendid beauty; but the light only served to show the boy his own lonesomeness and desolation, as he sat, with bleeding feet and covered with dust, upon a cold door-step. . . .

. . . He had been crouching on the step for some time: wondering at the great number of public-houses (every other house in Barnet was a tavern, large or small), gazing listlessly at the coaches as they passed through, and thinking how strange it seemed that they could do, with ease, in a few hours, what it had taken him a whole week of courage and determination beyond his years to accomplish: when he was roused by observing that a boy, who had passed him carelessly some minutes before, had returned, and was now surveying him most earnestly from the opposite side of the way.

CHARLES DICKENS, *Oliver Twist*, 1837–8

ACKNOWLEDGEMENTS

We would like to thank our families and friends who have helped us over the years during the preparation of this book, especially Sandy Marriage, Robin Ollington, Bryan Rooney, Suzanne St Albans, Anthony Sampson, Kathleen Tillotson, Malcolm Holmes of the Camden Local History Library and the staff of the North Reading Room, British Library.

The compilers and publishers gratefully acknowledge permission to reproduce the following copyright material in this book:

Hilaire Belloc: *More Peers*, © Hilaire Belloc 1911. Reprinted by permission of Peters, Fraser & Dunlop.

John Betjeman: 'Business Girls' (*A Few Late Chrysanthemums* 1954) and 'Parliament Hill Fields', 'South London Sketch' (*New Bats in Old Belfries* 1945) from *Collected Poems*. © John Betjeman 1958. *Summoned by Bells*, © John Betjeman 1960. Reprinted by permission of John Murray.

Angela Carter: in *Living in London* edited by Alan Ross, © Angela Carter 1974. Reprinted by permission of London Magazine.

Charlie Chaplin: *My Autobiography*, © Charlie Chaplin 1964. Reprinted by permission of The Bodley Head.